HASSAN GAI

C000090515

THE
CONCEPT OF
GOD
IN ISLAM

THE ISLAMIC FOUNDATION
THE NEW MUSLIMS PROJECT

British Library Cataloguing in Publication Data

Eaton, Hassan Gai
The concept of God in Islam
1.God (Islam) I.Title II.Islamic Foundation (Great Britain)
297.2'11

ISBN 08603703797

In the Name of Allah the Beneficent, the Merciful

Acknowledgement

IN HIS QUEST to find a niche – a place where he felt he 'belonged' Gai Eaton choose "*Dar-ul-Islam*, the house of Islam. From then on his passport here and in the hereafter was to be the simple Confession of Faith, *La ilaha illa 'Llah*," There is no god but God! In spite of the fact that "religion, it was assumed, had nothing to do with the more important studies which formed the backbone" of his early education an intense hunger consumed him as he struggled, hindered by what he saw as his own "ignorance as though immobilised in a dense fog,' to know the 'meaning of his own existence." It is clear, from his literary work, *The Richest Vein* which encompasses his early interest in philosophy and later mysticism, that this was a personal journey which was to meander its way throughout his life. *King of the Castle* subtitled '*Choice and Responsibility in the Modern World*' was published some years after his conversion to Islam and was later followed by *Islam and the Destiny of Man* and *Remembering God – Reflections on Islam* published in 2000.

The impact of this title, 'The Concept of God in Islam,' is no less powerful today as my first encounter with it in the early stages of my conversion to Islam some twenty five years ago. The author, who considers his own path to have been 'long and tortuous,' certainly, through this essay which appeared for the first time in the late seventies and his subsequent publications, made that special relationship we all crave with an innate sense and desire to be brought back to the origins and purpose of our own creation, an easier one to establish as well as to sustain for many. I would like to express our sincere thanks to Gai Eaton for allowing the New Muslims Project to reproduce this piece of work, which I believe to be one of great beauty, that it may continue to inspire those in search of their roots which are to be 'found in That which alone endures' – God the Creator and Sustainer of all things.

Those who believe and whose hearts are at rest in the remembrance of God – truly it is in the remembrance of God that hearts find rest. Qur'ān 13:28

Batool Al-Toma
New Muslims Project

Transliteration Table

Consonants. Arabic

initial: unexpressed medial and final:

ء	ʾ	د	d	ض	ḍ	ك	k
ب	b	ذ	dh	ط	ṭ	ل	l
ت	t	ر	r	ظ	ẓ	م	m
ث	th	ز	z	ع	ʿ	ن	n
ج	j	س	s	غ	gh	ـه	h
ح	ḥ	ش	sh	ف	f	و	w
خ	kh	ص	ṣ	ق	q	ي	y

Vowels, diphthongs, etc.

Short: ﹷ a   ﹻ i   ﹹ u

long: ـَا ā   ﹻي ī   ـُو ū

diphthongs: ـَوْ aw

              ـَىْ ay

The Concept of God in Islam

⟫

THE FIRST PART of the Muslim confession of faith (the *shahadah*) is the basis for the concept of God in Islam. The Muslim bears witness that: "There is no god but God", or "no divinity but the (*one*) Divinity". The revealed Scripture of Islam, the Qur'ān is like a vast commentary on this simple statement, drawing from it all its implications for human life and thought.

This conception of the Deity is strictly monotheistic and unitarian. God alone has absolute *being*, totally independent and totally self-sufficient. Whatever exists or ever could exist does so by His will. He has no "partner" either in creating the universe or in maintaining it in existence. He is not only the "First Cause" but also ultimately, the only cause, and He is Himself uncaused. The Qur'ān tells us: "Say: He is Allah, One, the utterly Self-sufficient; He begets not neither is He begotten, and there is nothing that is like unto Him". It tells us also that: "When He wills a thing to be, He but says unto it – Be!; and it is".

A further implication of the first part of the *shahadah* is that there can be no power, force or agency in the heavens or on earth which is independent of God. Everything that exists – and everything that happens – is subject to His control; there is nothing that can compete with Him or that escapes His grasp, nothing that does not bear witness to His creative power and majesty. "The seven heavens and the earth and all that is therein praise Him" says the Qur'ān, "and there is not a thing that does not hymn His praise, though ye understand not their praise".

In the Islamic view, it is impossible for the human mind to form an adequate conception of God as He is in His eternal and absolute being. The creature cannot comprehend the Creator. According to the Qur'ān, "No (human) vision encompasseth Him, yet He encompasseth (all) vision".

But Islam does not demand blind belief. The Qur'ān tells us a great deal about the nature of the Divine, and it describes God by a number of terms – called "the most beautiful Names" – which help us to understand Him. The Qur'ān tells us: "Allah, there is no god but He, the Living, the eternally Self-subsistent. Slumber overtakes Him not, nor sleep. To Him belong all that is in the heavens and all that is upon earth. Who is there than (can) intercede with Him except by His leave? He knows what is before them and what is behind them, and they comprehend naught of His knowledge save what He pleases. His Throne extends over the heavens and the earth, and He is not wearied by preserving them; and He is the Most High, the Immense".

He is **Al-Ahad, The One**, absolute unity. This is in sharp contrast to the Christian conception of the Trinity. The One cannot be divided, nor can it be diminished or "humanised" by incarnation in any created from. God does not become His own creature, in fact He does not "become" anything; He *is*.

The Qur'ān describes Him also as **Al-ʿAlī, the Most High,** totally transcendent in relation to His own creations and therefore infinitely beyond all that we might attempt to associate with Him. He is **Al-ʿAzīz, the Almighty** and **Al-Jabbār, the Irresistible,** for there is no one and nothing that could possibly resist His power, which governs and regulates all existence in accordance with a predetermined measure. It follows that there is no earthly power that is not derived from Him, no strength nor any virtue that is not loaned to us by Him; and no one can help us except by His will, nor can anyone harm us unless He permits them to do so (in which case this harm is a trial to be borne with patience).

He is called **Al-Haqq, the Truth** (or **the Reality**), and to deny Him is to be far distant from truth at every level of experience. The Arabic word for such "deniers" (or "unbelievers") is **Al-Kāfirūn**, and this word suggests a deliberate act of "covering"; in other words those who deny Him whose name is "the Truth" have "covered" their own understanding with an opaque covering so as not to see what is ultimately self-evident. In so doing they have shut out the light, for another of His names is **An-Nūr, Light**. These are they whom the Qur'ān describes as the "blind", for "Allah is the Light of the heavens and the earth". In Islam everything is derived from the divine nature and therefore from the "names" by which God has made Himself known, and if He were not "Light" there could be no light anywhere, whether intellectual or physical.

Nothing escapes His knowledge, not even our most secret thoughts for He is **Al-ʿAlīm, the Omniscient** who knows everything in the heavens and the earth, and **Al-Khabīr, the All-Aware"** from whom nothing is hidden. He is **Ash-Shahīd, the Witness** and, as such, He is described also as **Al-Basīr, the Seer** and **As-Samīʿ, the Hearer.** "Who is the Owner of hearing and of sight?" asks the Qur'ān, and it answers "Allah!" We see only what is before our eyes, with their very limited range, but no limit is set to His vision; we hear only sounds that are either very loud or very close to us, but He hears everything. "And with Him are the keys of the Invisible", says the Qur'ān. "None but He knoweth them, and He knoweth what is in the land and the sea. Not a leaf falls but He knoweth it, nor a grain amidst the darkness of the earth…".

He is **Al-Awwal, the First** before whom there is nothing, and **Al-Akhīr, the Last**, after whom there is nothing; but He is not only at the beginning and at the end of time, for He is also **Az-Zahīr, the**

Outward, present behind all the shifting scenes we perceive in the world around us, and **Al-Bātin, the Inward,** for it is His power that moves and motivates all that exists.

He is not only **Al-Khāliq, the Creator,** who gives each separate thing the light of existence by His command "Be!", but He is also **Al-Musawwir** who "*shapes*" it in accordance with the nature He wishes it to have, for everything in the world has its purpose and is moulded to serve that purpose.

When creatures have been brought into existence and fashioned in accordance with the divine purpose, they are not abandoned and left to fend for themselves. Two very particular "names" stand at the very centre of the Islamic concept of God. These are **Ar-Rahmān and Ar-Rahīm.** Both are derived from the Arabic word for "Mercy", **Rahma,** which is closely related to the word for "womb" and therefore carries with it implications of creativeness and fecundity. In one of the inspired sayings in which God spoke to mankind through the Prophet Muhammad (*peace be upon him*) we are told that His "Mercy" takes precedence over His "Wrath".

There are different opinions as to the exact distinction between the names **Ar-Rahmān** and **Ar-Rahīm** (which are placed at the beginning of all but one of the chapters of the Qur'ān). The former is usually translated as **the Merciful** and the latter as **the Compassionate.** It is said that the former describes God as He is in His eternal nature and that everything is brought into existence through the overflowing of this innate "Mercy", while the latter – **Ar-Rahīm** – refers to the blessings He pours out upon His creatures.

In whatever way we translate these words, the essential concept is not in doubt. God is infinitely merciful, first in giving us life and the means to enjoy life, secondly in caring for us and satisfying our legitimate needs. This concept is amplified by other divine names contained in the Qur'ān. God is described as **Al-Karīm, the Generous,** and as **Al-Wadūd, the Loving-Kind**; He is also **Ar-Razzāq, the Provider** who nourishes us both spiritually and physically.

Despite this outpouring of mercy, we still go astray, for man – as the Qur'ān tells us – was "created weak", and our situation might seem hopeless if God were not **At-Tawwāb, the Relenting,** who never tires of turning back to His creatures when they turn to him is repentance. He is **Al-Ghafūr, the Ever-Forgiving**, and **Al-ʿAfu, the Effacer (of sins)**. Whatever people may do in the course of their lives they have the opportunity to seek this forgiveness so long as they have breath, but the opportunity is lost when death comes and, after that, they are judged for what they are or for what they have made of themselves. So the Qur'ān says: "O My servants who have damaged your own selves despair not of the Mercy of Allah. Truly Allah pardons all sins. Truly He is the Forgiving, the Merciful. So turn unto your Lord repentant and surrender unto Him before the punishment comes upon you; then ye will not be helped".

But "sinning" and "going astray" would have no clear meaning if God had not shown His creatures the right way, the "straight path" as it is called in the Qur'ān. One of His names is **Al-Hādi, the Guide.** We are assured that He has never left any nation or any group of people without guidance; to each He has sent a "messenger" to deliver them a "message" of hope and guidance and to instruct them as to how to follow the "straight way" which leads to Paradise and, ultimately, to **Ar-Ridwān, the Good Pleasure** or **Satisfaction** of God Himself. These divine "messages" have been clothed in the language and thought-patterns of the people to whom they were addressed so as to be clear and unambiguous, and the "messengers" who have been the instruments of this guidance have been men like other men, though in every way better than others.

In spite of their clarity, these "messages" have again and again been rejected by many of those to whom they were addressed, and it is precisely this freedom to reject the truth that distinguishes man from the other creatures who share the earth with us – the animals, the birds and the fishes. They follow by instinct the way set before them, the law of their species, but mankind has the unique freedom either to follow the "straight path" consciously and deliberately or to turn away from it and follow the dictates of self-will. Man alone has been given a mind capable of understanding the truth, a will capable of choosing the path of truth, and a heart inclined by its very nature to love the truth.

"For each of you have We appointed a divine Law and a way of life," says the Qur'ān; "Had Allah so willed, He could have made you one people; but so that He may try you by that which He hath bestowed upon you, (He hath willed otherwise). So compete in doing good. Unto Allah ye will all return, and He will inform you regarding that wherein ye differ". In terms of this and other similar verses, it is entirely possible for Muslims to accept the idea that the pre-Islamic religions were at least partial statements of the One Truth, adapted to time and place and to the spiritual needs of different peoples.

The Muslim however believes that the message brought by the Prophet Muḥammad (*peace be upon him*) completes that vast structure of revelation and provides a final synthesis, after which there is nothing more to be said. Judaism and Christianity are both "monotheistic" religions, but Muslims consider that the Jews appropriated the universal Truth, claiming it as the property of one single people, while the Christians redefined it through the doctrines of the Trinity and the Incarnation. In the Islamic view, the "message" transmitted through Muḥammad (*peace be upon him*) represented, not a completely new religion, but a corrective to the falsifications and distortions which had taken place and, at the same time, an uncompromising re-assertion of the pure doctrine of the One God.

According to the Islamic concept, God demands of us three things. The first is a constant awareness of Him, even in the midst of our worldly

activities. This awareness is expressed in two words which constantly recur in the Qur'ān. *Taqwa* is commonly translated either as "fear of God" or "God consciousness"; both translations are acceptable, since we cannot be truly "conscious" of Him without experiencing a profound sense of awe which results in a healthy fear of displeasing Him or offending against His laws. The Arabic word *dhikr*, meaning both "mention" and "remembrance", has a more devotional connotation, and we are assured that God is present with us when we "remember" Him or "mention" His name. Although Islam lays a great emphasis on the divine transcendence, the Qur'ān speaks on many occasions of the "closeness" of God to His believing servants: "He is with you wheresoever you may be", and "we are closer to him (man) than his jugular vein". We read also in the Qur'ān that "it is in the remembrance (*dhikr*) of Allah that hearts find rest".

Secondly, He demands of us that we should obey His commandments, which are in no way arbitrary; whether we know it or not, they are for our own good and are, therefore, an aspect of the divine Mercy. Their purpose is to maintain a healthy balance both within the human personality and in society and, at the same time, to provide a stable framework for human living. In Islam God is the only Legislator or Lawgiver. We cannot legislate effectively for ourselves since our laws would inevitably be designed in accordance with our short-term desires. From the commands and prohibitions contained in the Qur'ān and from the teachings and example of the Prophet Muḥammad (*peace be upon him*) is derived the *Shari'ah*, the Law which governs every aspect of the Muslim's life on earth.

Finally, since we are by nature weak and inclined to self-indulgence, God demands of us sincere repentance when we have failed to live up to what He requires of us. Muslim's recognize that our weakness, however much we may deplore it, has a positive aspect, for if we were strong we would be tempted to see ourselves as self-reliant little "gods" quite independent of our Creator. Being weak by nature we soon find that we cannot rely either upon ourselves or upon other people and this obliges us to turn to Him whom the Qur'ān describes as **Al-Wakil, the Utterly Reliable.** "There is no power and no strength except with Allah", according to one of Muḥammad's (pbuh) favourite savings.

The unfolding of human destinies, obedient or disobedient, as the case may be, takes place against a meaningful background. In the Islamic view, God creates nothing without a purpose. "Do you not see", says the Qur'ān "that Allah hath created the heavens and the earth with (and by) the Truth?" The whole universe is filled – like a great picture-book –with "signs" which bear witness to its creator and which reminds us, if we have pure hearts and seeing eyes, of His power. His majesty and His beauty. The Qur'ān tells us: "Indeed, in the heavens and the earth are signs for believers, and in your creation and in all the beasts that He has scattered upon the earth are signs for people whose faith is sure; and in the difference of night and day and in the provision that Allah sendeth down from the heavens and thereby quickeneth the earth after her death – and in the ordering of the winds – are signs for people of understanding".

This serves to emphasize an essential element in the Islamic conception of God. Our existence and the existence of the whole universe around us are proofs of God, and this is cogently expressed in another passage from the Qur'ān: "We shall show them Our signs on the horizons and within themselves until it is clear to them that this is the truth. Doth not thy lord suffice thee. since He is witness over all things? And so – are they still in doubt about the meeting with their Lord? Doth He not indeed encompass all things?"

To sum up: the God of Islam is transcendent, the all-powerful and all-knowing Creator and Lawgiver, though at the same time infinitely

merciful, generous and forgiving. Man, His creature and His servant into whom He has breathed something of His spirit, stands before Him without intermediary or intercessor, meeting Him through prayer during this brief life on earth and meeting Him face-to-face when life is over. In Islam, God does not embody Himself in any human being or make Himself accessible through idols and images.

But he **does** make Himself accessible through His revealed Names. We, in our small way, can exemplify these qualities and attributes in our daily lives. Inspired and aided by **the Most Merciful** we can show mercy. Inspired and aided by **the One who creates Guidance** we can guide our fellow men and women. Through His Light our lives may be illuminated. What we cannot hope to exemplify fully is His Perfection, but we can love it whole-heartedly. We love those who are kind to us, and **God is Kindness** itself. We love generosity when it is directed towards us, and He is **the Selflessly Generous One.** We are irresistibly drawn towards beauty, and He is the source of all Beauty. Above all, we love Perfection, and we seek it in vain in this imperfect world. We find it in God, who is alone perfect, and the Qur'ān tells us that "the believers are strong in their love of God". At the end of the road, sign-posted by the divine Names, the Muslim rejoices in an overwhelming love for the One who awaits us at journey's end.

NOTES

1. 'There is no God but Allah and Muḥammad (peace be upon him) is His Prophet'.

2. 'Oh the Merciful'.

3. 'He is the ever Living and Self Subsisting One'.

4. 'Oh Lord, give me ease with bounty and not difficulty'.

5. 'There is no God but He'.

6. 'Oh messenger we have sent you as a witness, a giver of glad tidings and a warner'.